11-30-19

The Promise and Perils of Technology™

ARTIFICIAL INTELLIGENCE AND YOU

Corona Brezina

New York

Published in 2020 by The Rosen Publishing Group, Inc.
29 East 21st Street, New York, NY 10010

Copyright © 2020 by The Rosen Publishing Group, Inc.

First Edition

All rights reserved. No part of this book may be reproduced in any form without permission in writing from the publisher, except by a reviewer.

Library of Congress Cataloging-in-Publication Data

Names: Brezina, Corona, author.
Title: Artificial intelligence and you / Corona Brezina.
Description: New York, NY : The Rosen Publishing Group, Inc., 2020. | Series: The promise and perils of technology | Includes bibliographical references and index. | Audience: Grades 7–12.
Identifiers: LCCN 2018043294| ISBN 9781508188193 (library bound) | ISBN 9781508188186 (pbk.)
Subjects: LCSH: Artificial intelligence—Juvenile literature.
Classification: LCC TA347.A78 B74 2020 | DDC 006.3—dc23
LC record available at https://lccn.loc.gov/2018043294

Manufactured in the United States of America

CONTENTS

	Introduction	4
1	Introducing Artificial Intelligence	6
2	The History of AI	16
3	AI in Everyday Life	24
4	AI in the Workplace	33
5	The Future of AI	42
	Glossary	49
	For More Information	52
	For Further Reading	56
	Bibliography	57
	Index	61

INTRODUCTION

In March 2017, the artificial intelligence (AI) computer program AlphaGo defeated the top-ranked human Go player, Lee Sedol, after winning four out of five games. The ancient Chinese game of Go is much more complicated than chess, and observers were stunned that the AI could achieve the victory.

The landmark defeat was not the first high-profile win for an AI competing against a top human player. In 1997, the chess-playing IBM system Deep Blue had defeated chess master Garry Kasparov. In 2011, an IBM AI called Watson won the TV trivia game *Jeopardy!* over two top players.

After each instance, public debate arose over whether machines had finally become smarter than humans. Skeptics would point out that although the computer programs were very intelligent in a specific domain, they possessed less general intelligence than a human toddler.

AI pioneer John McCarthy defined AI as "the science and engineering of making intelligent machines, especially intelligent computer programs," as archived on his Stanford website. Nonetheless, many experts in the field disagree on a precise definition of AI. Intelligence itself is difficult to define, even for humans. Measuring your IQ is not a full description of your intelligence, which also encompasses aspects such as judgment, communication skills, and emotions. In addition, machine intelligence is not directly comparable to human intelligence.

Although AI is nowhere near approaching human-level intelligence, narrow applications of AI are already common in your daily life. You experience AI using apps on your smartphone, playing video games, and getting music or movie recommendations on your computer. Every day brings new stories of AI breakthroughs, from AI potential in diagnosing diseases to a project led by teenage girls who are putting AI tools to work in predicting incidents of gun violence.

Some experts predict a bright future enhanced by AI. The technology has the potential to relieve human workers of some of the

IBM's Watson (*center*) holds an advantage against human contestants Ken Jennings (*left*) and Brad Rutter (*right*) during a press conference before the 2011 "Man Versus Machine" *Jeopardy!* competition.

dangerous and repetitive aspects of their jobs. In an age of "big data," AI could help analyze and organize information, leading to increased productivity in many industries. But AI also brings concerns over jobs that could be lost to automation, biased algorithms leading to discrimination, and loss of privacy protection. Emerging AI applications—from self-driving cars to facial recognition software to robotic process automation software in offices—are prompting discussion of how the technology brings risks as well as benefits.

CHAPTER 1

Introducing Artificial Intelligence

AI is a broad field that draws on many different areas of study. The circuits and hardware of AI machines are designed by mechanical and electrical engineers. Researchers employ psychology, the study of the mind and human behavior, and neuroscience, the field that examines how the brain and nervous system function. The discipline of philosophy provides valuable tools in areas such

At Google's annual I/O developers conference in Mountain View, California, participants can attend a coding lab on creating software for the company's AI-based voice assistant.

Introducing Artificial Intelligence

as probability, logic, and reasoning, which can be used in designing how an AI approaches a problem. Philosophical debate can also address more abstract issues regarding AI, such as whether an AI can achieve human-level intelligence or possess a mind. Other relevant areas include linguistics, statistics, and economics.

The single discipline most essential to AI, however, is computer science. AI is largely the realm of computer programmers.

Programming a Thinking Machine

AI machines function by using algorithms and processing data. An algorithm is a sequence of steps that solve a problem. The data that is stored and analyzed by AI can be either structured—organized in a searchable database, for example—or unstructured. Unstructured data is information in formats such as text files, audio, images, and videos.

One of the most famous AI programs, IBM's Watson, was provided with numerous types of data such as encyclopedias, dictionaries, and news sources in preparation for its 2011 *Jeopardy!* appearance. But to answer the trivia questions, Watson also had to understand what was being asked, retrieve relevant information, and use reasoning to select the correct answer. When asked a question, Watson executed algorithms to perform these processes.

There are many facets to human intelligence, and AI is more successful in simulating some types than others. As demonstrated by programs that play games such as chess, AI can outperform humans in some areas that involve thinking logically. Humans also use several forms of intelligence to perceive and interact with the environment around them. Comparable AI applications include devices such as robotic arms and facial recognition software. Another key element of human intelligence is linguistic ability. AI is not yet capable of simulating human written and verbal communication—

Artificial Intelligence and You

A new owner of an iPhone X sets up facial recognition authentication technology utilizing AI that enables him to unlock the phone, make purchases, and sign in to apps.

Watson can answer trivia questions, for example, but it cannot hold a conversation. Finally, AI does not have the potential for creativity or intrapersonal intelligence (self-reflection), which are key aspects of human intelligence.

In some ways, AI analyses are similar to human thought processes. An AI machine receives data, interprets it, and works toward achieving goals. AI is capable of reasoning, planning, learning, and solving problems. Some AI machines can draw on knowledge, perceive their environment through sensory inputs, and manipulate objects around them.

Introducing Artificial Intelligence

When describing AI abilities, experts sometimes differentiate between human and rational performance. Humans don't always think or behave rationally. People may make decisions based on instincts or mood instead of analyzing the best possible outcome. Depending on the scenario, programmers may aim to create an AI that acts or thinks rationally, or, alternately, mimics how a human acts or thinks.

AI can be narrow—intended for a specific purpose—or generalized, in which it can manage a greater range of tasks. This concept is sometimes described as weak versus strong AI. Present-day AI qualifies as weak AI: it performs a specific task, such as speech recognition or playing a game. Watson is brilliant at answering questions, but Watson is limited to answering questions. Strong AI, sometimes called artificial general intelligence (AGI) is a hypothetical AI that achieves genuine human-level intelligence—or greater—across a range of different types of tasks.

There are many branches of AI, and they frequently overlap. Two key subfields are symbolic reasoning and neural networks. Symbolic reasoning is based on a system of rules. Knowledge is represented as symbols that are organized into collections that can be manipulated to solve problems. IBM's Deep Blue machine, which proved AI superiority in chess in 1997, utilized symbolic reasoning. Neural networks, by contrast, are based on the connections of neurons in the human brain. A web of nodes working together solves problems by detecting patterns. The program AlphaGo incorporated neural networks.

Machine learning is another area in AI with exciting potential. In much the same way that humans learn, AI programs can improve performance through experience or training. One cutting-edge type of machine learning, deep learning, emerged during the early twenty-first century. Deep learning systems process data by passing it through multiple layers of a neural network.

Researchers are also pursuing a variety of areas in AI relevant to practical issues in people's everyday lives. AI planners generate

Artificial Intelligence and You

The Turing Test

Can a machine truly possess intelligence? In 1950, computer pioneer Alan Turing devised a test in which a computer and a human being, both unseen, would answer an interrogator's questions for five minutes. The machine passes the Turing test, as it is now called, if the judge cannot identify which responses were human.

There have been many criticisms of the Turing test. Some claim that it can be fooled by trickery on the part of computer programmers. Others question whether the ability to hold a conversation is proof of genuine intelligence. Alternate intelligence tests for machines have been devised, such as cognitive scientist Stevan Harnad's Total Turing Test. The Total Turing Test requires that the machine also be able to see and interact in its physical environment.

a sequence of steps toward a goal, such as giving directions or putting together equipment. Machine vision makes it possible for AI programs and devices to interpret real-world images. Speech recognition enables AI to understand what you're saying. A wider subfield, natural language processing, deals with AI capabilities for manipulating language, both written and spoken.

Incorporating Hardware

AI also overlaps with the field of robotics. Many people primarily associate the concept of AI with robots as they are depicted in science fiction. You may have seen the robot Rosey on the cartoon *The Jetsons*, read about sophisticated robots in the stories of science fiction writer Isaac Asimov, or followed the adventures of R2-D2 and C-3PO in

Introducing Artificial Intelligence

the *Star Wars* movies. Some of these futuristic predictions from the past have come true. Like Rosey the maid, robots with roles in the workforce are expected to take on unskilled, repetitive jobs that can easily be automated. Many of Asimov's characters grapple with the ethical and legal implications of AI existing alongside humans in society. Although C-3PO is highly knowledgeable, he often demonstrates a lack of understanding of human motivations.

However, fictional robots tend to resemble human beings, and some even have superhuman characteristics. They possess capabilities such as moving, reasoning, and communicating without supervision from humans.

This depiction is inaccurate on two levels. AI and robotics are two separate fields that sometimes overlap. Robots are machines that can perform tasks with some degree of autonomy, meaning

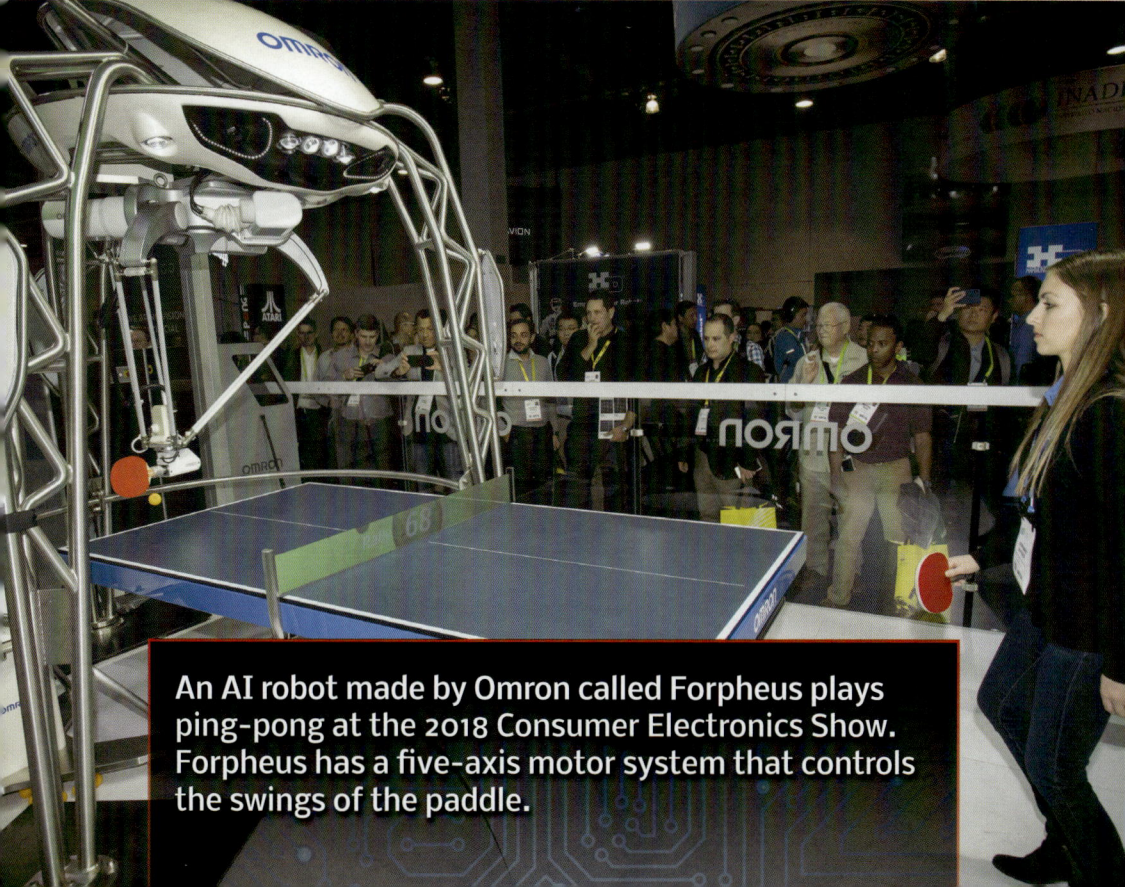

An AI robot made by Omron called Forpheus plays ping-pong at the 2018 Consumer Electronics Show. Forpheus has a five-axis motor system that controls the swings of the paddle.

Artificial Intelligence and You

that they aren't being directly controlled by humans. Robots are programmed to follow instructions, but they do not necessarily possess artificial intelligence. In addition, most AI does not involve robotic components. Like Watson and Deep Blue, most of the AI you're likely to encounter in your daily life exists as software.

Nonetheless, robots are getting smarter, and researchers are expanding the capabilities of AI to interact with their environment. Advances in computing hardware has enabled AI to process more information at faster speeds. AI equipped with specialized cameras, microphones, and sensors can collect data about its surroundings. AI robots already perform tasks in some settings, such as factory work and health care. Self-driving cars and some drones also possess AI, and these mobile AI machines may become more common in the future. Researchers for many companies and institutions are also pursuing development of AI robots that resemble human beings. So far, however, these humanoid robots are mainly research projects or curiosities with little practical purpose.

Benefits and Drawbacks of AI

One of the most pressing present-day concerns regarding AI is how its growth will affect people's jobs. There are many different projected scenarios about whether AI will help or hurt the workforce. AI could potentially replace human workers across many different areas of work, forcing people to seek jobs in new fields. Alternately, growth in AI could be complemented by increased demand for employees to work alongside AI machines, especially in fields such as education and health care.

If you read news stories about advances in AI, you might be tempted to believe that AI devices are certain to win in the workplace. AI machines and software have been developed that can flip burgers, write news articles, and perform administrative work in offices.

Introducing Artificial Intelligence

An Uber self-driving car navigates the streets of San Francisco, California, in 2017. In response to the new technology, many states have passed laws related to autonomous vehicles.

Customers in stores can have their purchases continually monitored by AI cameras as they shop, eliminating the need for a cashier. Fleets of self-driving trucks could put millions of truck drivers out of work. AI could continue to increase the efficiency of robots in factories, leading to the loss of more manufacturing jobs to automation. But the existence of these AI capabilities does not mean that they will

13

be widely adopted in the near future. Although AI will continue to become more common, implementation is likely to be gradual. Your neighborhood grocery store, for example, won't be replacing cashiers with expensive and experimental AI scanners any time soon.

AI is also raising issues concerning security and privacy. A drone or a closed-circuit television (CCTV) system equipped with AI capabilities could conceivably alert the authorities if it observed what it was programmed to label a suspicious situation. Facial recognition software could mean that anytime you're photographed in a public place, you could conceivably be identified by anyone who possesses the technology. Some workplaces extensively monitor employees to assess job performance. But as AI surveillance capabilities grow more powerful, people have begun asking questions about potential abuses of power and basic privacy rights.

In the mid-term future, humans may need to give serious consideration as to how to coexist with AI. On March 19, 2018, an Arizona woman became the first person to be hit and killed by a self-driving vehicle, an Uber car. Her family reached a settlement with Uber. But the issue of crashes involving self-driving cars—as well as any AI that performs an action that would be a crime if committed by a human—could raise moral and legal questions in the future. A self-driving car could conceivably encounter a situation where any action taken would injure a human, for example. Programmers will have to design algorithms to enable self-driving cars to deal with contingencies. Yet, how should they formulate instructions for an AI regarding what is mainly a moral dilemma? Furthermore, if a self-driving car does injure or kill someone, who is held responsible—the car's owner, the corporation that designed the car, or the AI?

AI could also eventually affect relationships and social interactions. Parents already worry about the effects of too much screen time for their children. Exchanges on social media can affect friendships. Communication with AI could lead to even more time spent using electronic devices and potentially less time spent in the company of other people. Users could even come to prefer using

Introducing Artificial Intelligence

AI in some contexts. As a result, they wouldn't have to deal with human elements such as careless mistakes or emotional reactions. People might contact an AI for help in scenarios when they would formerly have called a friend or family member. AI probably won't cause communities or societies to crumble, but it could change some of the conventions of how people communicate.

In the far-off future, people may have to address the ethical and philosophical implications of machines that have achieved human-level intelligence. If an AI can move, act, feel, and demonstrate the creativity of a person, should it be granted legal rights? Conceivably, human beings could be enhanced with robotic and AI parts someday, and humanoid AI robots could be equipped with biological body parts. These scenarios could change the definition of what it means to be human. Should humans be worried about the "singularity," the technology that potentially enables AI to overtake humans in intelligence and break free from human control? These are wildly speculative notions, but in a world that's being constantly transformed by cutting-edge technology, they're worth considering.

CHAPTER 2

The History of AI

The term "artificial intelligence" was coined in the twentieth century, but the concept of manmade objects brought to life is ancient. Throughout history, human mythology and literature have described various human creations that are capable of thinking and feeling. In the Greek myth of Pygmalion and Galatea, for example, the sculptor Pygmalion carves a marble statue of the perfect woman. He ends up falling in love with his own creation. Aphrodite, the goddess of love, observes Pygmalion's passion and brings Galatea to life.

The myth was updated with an AI twist in the 1995 novel *Galatea 2.2*, by Richard Powers. The narrator is charged with training an AI neural network program named Helen to produce literary criticism that is difficult to tell apart from the work of a human. Powers explores the nature of both human and artificial intelligence and consciousness.

Today, it seems that AI could be on the verge of achieving new breakthroughs and transforming how people live and work. But history shows that grandiose predictions about the future of AI often turn out to be hype.

Computer scientist John McCarthy of Stanford University moves chess pieces in a game being played between a Soviet computer and an American computer in 1966. Countermoves had already been inputted into the computers' programs.

The History of AI

Origins at the Dartmouth Workshop

The discipline of artificial intelligence had its origins in a summer conference held in 1956 at Dartmouth College, in Hanover, New Hampshire. John McCarthy, then a Dartmouth professor, invited a small group of researchers to the Dartmouth Workshop to discuss the possibility of creating machines that could simulate human intelligence. McCarthy was a renowned computer scientist who is now considered one of the founders of the field. He invented the term "artificial intelligence" during the course of the workshop. He also invented the programming language LISP that was dominant in AI for decades and is still used in some versions.

Another organizer of the conference was the legendary AI pioneer Marvin Minsky. He performed substantial research into AI, wrote extensively on the subject, and cofounded the Massachusetts Institute of Technology (MIT) Artificial Intelligence Project with McCarthy in 1959. Minsky remained at MIT for the rest of his career; McCarthy moved on to Stanford University in Stanford, California, where he founded the Stanford Artificial Intelligence Laboratory.

Several other participants in the Dartmouth Conference also made notable achievements in AI and computer science. Herbert Simon and Allen Newell, professors at Carnegie Mellon University in Pittsburgh, Pennsylvania, invented an early AI program that they called the Logical Theorist, which they presented at the Dartmouth Workshop. Simon's research into decision making and problem solving cut across disciplines including economics, political science, computer science, and psychology. He won the Nobel Prize for Economics in 1978. Newell established a prestigious career in computer science, notable particularly for his work on the theory of cognition. Other prominent participants included Claude Shannon, who founded the discipline of information theory, Oliver Selfridge, who performed groundbreaking AI research on machine perception, and Nathaniel Rochester, who helped design IBM's first computer.

Some topics of discussion at the Dartmouth Workshop remain highly relevant in AI. According to the proposal for the conference (as archived on McCarthy's website), the researchers aimed to "find how to make machines use language, form abstractions and concepts, solve kinds of problems now reserved for humans, and improve themselves." They debated how to define the new discipline and discussed topics such as neural nets and language processing. They also made some optimistic predictions for the future of AI development. Simon, in particular, believed that it wouldn't take long to develop machines that could do the work of human beings.

The History of AI

Breakthroughs and Winters

Simon's expectations of AI began a pattern of overly bright predictions for advances in the field. The history of AI has alternated between periods of progress and "winters," in which support and funding stalled, often because of disappointing results that didn't live up to expectations.

The Dartmouth Workshop spurred interest in AI, and researchers began making progress with machines that think. In 1958, Frank Rosenblatt created an early neural network that he called the perceptron. Machine learning was introduced in 1959 with the creation of a program that played checkers. In 1965, Joseph

Frank Rosenblatt's Mark I Perceptron is shown in the Cornell Aeronautical Laboratory in Buffalo, New York, around 1960. Rosenblatt based his model on the neural processes of the brain.

Artificial Intelligence and You

Weizenbaum, an MIT professor, debuted a program called ELIZA that would today be called a chatbot. ELIZA played the role of a psychotherapist during conversations with the user.

Also in 1965, researchers at Stanford began working on a program called DENDRAL, which used reasoning to analyze chemicals based on data about the substance. DENDRAL was the first "expert system"—a system that drew on a knowledge base to make decisions. Specialized expert systems became widespread by the early 1980s. The term "expert system" is not used much anymore, but the concepts are still incorporated into many AI applications.

In 1966, Shakey became the first robot to incorporate AI. A Stanford project that continued until 1972, Shakey could move around on wheels, perceive its surroundings, solve problems, and

DARPA and AI

In 1958, the US Department of Defense established the Advanced Research Projects Agency (now DARPA–the Defense Advanced Research Projects Agency) to support the development of innovative technology. One early project was the ARPANET, a forerunner to the internet. DARPA also invested heavily in AI research during the 1960s, particularly in the areas of natural language processing. DARPA provided funding for the robot Shakey (a robot with basic reasoning abilities) as well as AI programs at several other universities. After a lack of progress and a pair of pessimistic government reports, however, the government largely ceased funding AI in the early 1970s.

DARPA made AI history once again in the early 2000s, however, by funding the DARPA Grand Challenge that helped launch projects by automobile and tech companies to develop autonomous vehicles. Today, DARPA continues to fund cutting-edge AI research.

make plans. Shakey became famous—*Life* magazine declared it the "first electronic person" in 1970. But researchers remember being asked whether the technology could affect employment in the future.

Beginning in 1968, Terry Winograd developed SHRDLU, one of the first natural language processing programs, as his PhD thesis at MIT. The program could take part in dialogue in plain English and move around colored blocks with a robotic arm in response to commands. SHRDLU was an impressive demonstration, but follow-up work in natural language processing failed to make significant advances.

In 1969, Minsky, with Seymour Papert, published a controversial paper claiming that perceptrons were a highly limited form of AI. Subsequently, funding for neural networks dwindled. Research in the area stagnated until the 1980s. AI had not lived up to the hype, and government and commercial investment declined. A general "winter" for work in AI began in 1974. For the next couple of decades, periods of progress were followed by reduced funding and interest.

By the 1990s, however, advances in computing power and storage enabled new breakthroughs in AI. The 1997 defeat of chess champ Garry Kasparov by Deep Blue represented a major achievement in AI. Moreover, it thrust AI into the public spotlight.

The Age of Machine Learning

The AI resurgence of the twenty-first century has largely been the result of advances in machine learning. Machine learning is not a new concept in AI, but today's machines are much more sophisticated and can draw on a much larger pool of information. Watson, the computer that won *Jeopardy!* in 2011, utilized machine learning as well as other AI subfields.

Machine learning enables AI to make predictions based on training data rather than programming. There are several different

Artificial Intelligence and You

A neural network built by Google—consisting of sixteen thousand processors—taught itself to recognize cats. The project attempted to imitate the functioning of the brain.

categories of machine learning. Supervised learning consists of providing the machine with input data in which the output is already known—for example, classifying items into different groups. The machine learns how the input relates to the output and will be able to make predictions with new data. In unsupervised learning, the machine is provided with data that doesn't have a known result.

The History of AI

Instead, the machine is expected to discover relationships or patterns on its own. Supervised learning is more commonly used, while unsupervised learning is more complex and unpredictable. A newer type of machine learning is reinforcement learning, in which the machine learns through trial and error. The machine is given a reward signal when it returns the desired response.

Deep learning, which was developed during the 2010s, is the most novel form of machine learning. Deep learning involves filtering information through layers of a neural network made up of processing nodes. Information is passed from each individual node to multiple nodes in the next layer down, but the information is not shared among nodes in the same layer. Depending on the strength of the connections between nodes in upper layers, a node may or may not pass a piece of data to the next layer down. The final layer is called the output layer. The connections between nodes are self-adjusted during the learning process, yielding more consistent predictions.

In a renowned early example of deep learning, an AI learned in 2012 to recognize cats after viewing ten million random images taken from YouTube. The programmers had not provided the system with background information on cats or any other object category.

Because of twenty-first century advances in AI, people are now accustomed to AI capabilities in settings such as video games, smartphone platforms, and online commerce. One of the hottest areas of AI research and development is autonomous vehicles. The race to create a self-driving car began in earnest in 2004, when robot cars competed in the DARPA Grand Challenge, a 150-mile (241-kilometer) course through the Mojave Desert. None of the entries completed the course that year, but subsequent contests saw winners.

CHAPTER 3

AI in Everyday Life

It's very likely that you interact with AI in some of your day-to-day activities without even realizing it. Major breakthroughs in AI tend to make news headlines, but the introductions of AI in everyday activities has been subtler. Your video games, online shopping, and social media platforms all utilize AI capabilities. You've benefited from AI if you've planned your route with the assistance of online maps or used a ride-sharing service. As the technology grows more powerful and sophisticated, AI will continue to play a greater role in ordinary life.

Your AI Helpers and Friends

You're probably already familiar with virtual digital assistants such as Apple's Siri and Amazon's Alexa. They answer questions, manage your schedule, and perform tasks such as placing online orders. Virtual digital assistants use AI capabilities such as natural language processing and voice recognition. Some can learn to recognize the voices of multiple users. The programs also utilize machine learning to improve their responses based on past results. As the virtual digital assistant learns your preferences, it will display only options relevant to your request rather than the full range of possible results. Hundreds of millions of people worldwide use virtual digital assistants regularly. With such a huge audience, companies are sure to devote resources to improving and expanding their capabilities. Young people are part of the AI trend, according to a 2017 survey by

AI in Everyday Life

Smart products, such as Amazon Echo speakers with built-in Alexa Voice Service, incorporate microphones so that the user can give voice commands to the digital assistant.

the Pew Research Center. More than a third of respondents who were asked why they used voice-controlled digital assistants mentioned that the devices were easier for children to use.

AI also helps power social networking capabilities. Have you ever uploaded an image to a social media site and had the service tag your friends' faces in a photo to prompt you to identify them or offered similar images that might interest you? The service is probably using facial recognition or machine vision. When browsing online, are you provided with content and advertisements that are so relevant that they seem tailored just to your taste? Social media sites—as well as

A concertgoer uses a Sia selfie filter while attending a concert by the pop singer Sia in 2016—an example of AI providing fun special effects in everyday life.

AI in Everyday Life

many other online services—use AI to display content based on a user's past activity and specific demographics. These are just a few of the many examples of AI in social media. Instagram filters that enable you to edit facial features in an image utilize AI. LinkedIn, the career social networking site, matches job seekers to job openings using AI.

You've probably also encountered AI in video games. Unlike the programs that play games such as chess or Go, the AI in gaming is intended to improve the human player's experience. The most common role for AI is in nonplayer characters—the background characters who interact with the player's character but that aren't controlled by the player. The AI in video games is not always sophisticated, but nonplayer characters in some games can remember encounters, for example, and interact with their surroundings. In most cases, however, AI cannot learn from the player's actions and change its own behavior in response. Programming nonplayer characters that learn is complicated and can yield unpredictable results.

Companies use AI in many aspects of e-commerce and online service subscriptions, such as movies or music streaming. Shopping sites often return personalized search results, either tailored to your past history if you're signed in or based on the behavior of other customers. They may suggest products, offer discounts on specific items, or show you targeted ads. Similarly, services track your taste in music and movies to make recommendations. When you're almost ready to make a purchase, online retailers may also utilize customer support chatbots powered by AI to answer your questions about products or store policies.

The previous examples are mostly limited to online interactions, but AI is gradually entering the physical world as well. Most people are uneasy about the idea of robot babysitters, but some baby monitors incorporate cameras with AI facial recognition and motion detectors. Parents can buy their kids AI toys ranging from race cars to dolls, as well as robots and other devices that teach young people about the technology of AI. Devices and services powered by AI also have potential applications for helping people who are elderly remain healthy and independent. Sensors and monitors can detect falls and monitor medical conditions, for example. Social robots have been tested that interact with older adults as companions and help keep them connected to family and friends.

AI on the Road

AI is already changing the experience on the road. Even if you've never seen a self-driving car in person, the smart features on standard cars feature AI. Safety features such as automatic braking and collision avoidance technology are becoming more common. Newer vehicles may also have driver assist capabilities, such as steering assistance for parking and adaptive cruise control that changes speed depending on traffic conditions. In the future, your car may have AI sensors and cameras that monitor the driver and passengers. Technology under the hood may use AI to diagnose mechanical problems.

Ride sharing apps such as Uber and Lyft also utilize AI. The services track and analyze various types of data every time a customer takes a ride. They use the information to improve and refine performance in areas such as predicting wait time, managing demand, estimating fares, selecting drop-off locations, and choosing routes, especially to minimize detours when dropping off passengers.

The ultimate goal regarding AI in automobiles is, of course, autonomous cars. Ride sharing companies have already invested in the technology. So have major automobile manufacturers and newer companies established to develop high-tech vehicles, such as Waymo, an arm of Google's parent company, Alphabet Inc. Tesla is particularly advanced in cutting-edge features and updates that utilize AI. Self-driving cars employ machine learning to help vehicles learn to drive, cameras equipped with machine vision, lidar (light detection and ranging), radar to detect nearby objects, and highly detailed maps. But are the vehicles safe? Although advocates predict

AI in Everyday Life

US transportation secretary Elaine Chao (*right*) examines the lidar system on a self-driving car in 2017 while visiting an autonomous vehicle testing facility at the University of Michigan in Ann Arbor.

that autonomous cars will reduce traffic accidents by eliminating human error, the public remains distrustful.

AI could also assist with traffic management and safety on the roads. Computer vision can already read the license plates of vehicles caught by traffic cameras. The future could see smart traffic lights and other means of improving traffic flow. One day, a transition

Artificial Intelligence and You

AI and Mapping

Online mapping services have already replaced atlases and road maps. AI could add another layer of accessibility and personalization to maps. In 2018, Google offered a preview peek at its improved Maps product that makes use of AI machine vision and recommendations. Directions to locations are displayed over the view of the user's surroundings as seen on the screen through the camera. The recommendation service could direct users to restaurants and other places that match the user's preferences. A virtual assistant could eventually be introduced into the program.

Autonomous vehicles could also spur innovations in AI mapping. Multiple companies are developing highly detailed navigation guides for self-driving cars using a variety of different approaches to processing data.

to autonomous cars could bring an end to roadway congestion as vehicles work cooperatively to coordinate routes.

AI in Your Home

The internet of things (IoT) is made up of smart, connected devices that can collect and transmit a huge amount of data. It is not a new idea, but AI could take the IoT mainstream. "Smart homes" can be controlled remotely through smartphones or other devices. Appliances and systems such as light and heating learn your schedule and preferences. Devices such as speakers can be voice controlled by digital assistants. Safety and security measures, such as AI home security cameras and carbon monoxide detectors, can be accessed on smartphones.

AI in Everyday Life

Samsung Electronics demonstrates this refrigerator called the Family Hub, one of their smart appliances available in 2018 with a digital touchscreen and interior cameras that can connect to other home devices.

In the future, homes may be connected to a "smart grid." Assisted by AI, an electrical grid with improved communication capabilities would be more efficient and better able to respond to fluctuations in supply and demand. In particular, this capability could allow power companies to fully integrate renewable energy resources. They would be better prepared to handle the unpredictability of wind power,

31

for example, along with small-scale resources such as rooftop solar panels on homes. Improved communication would enable outages to be identified and fixed more quickly.

This proliferation of AI in people's daily lives—from digital assistants who know your personal preferences to smart homes that know your habits—represent significant privacy and security concerns. Even if you take common-sense precautions to protect your data, it is still stored and managed by tech companies, which may use it for numerous purposes that aren't always in your best interest. If a company experiences a security breach, such as being hacked and having user data stolen, you could risk consequences such as identity theft or fraud.

CHAPTER 4

AI in the Workplace

In a 2017 survey by the Pew Research Center, Americans shared opinions on the potential impact of advances in automation in their lives. The area of greatest concern was "a future in which robots and computers can perform many of the jobs currently done by human workers." Nearly three-quarters of respondents reported being worried by that possibility.

Experts disagree on the likelihood that AI and robots will transform the workplace of the future. Some emphasize the improvements in productivity that AI could bring. Others predict that AI and robots will cost human jobs. A 2018 report by an international forum, the Organisation for Economic Co-operation and Development (OECD), predicted that about 14 percent of jobs were threatened by automation—a lower figure than some previous studies. Nonetheless, the workers most at risk of losing their jobs were low-wage, low-skilled workers. This suggests the prospect that increased automation could lead to greater economic inequality.

AI Does Your Busy Work

Many office jobs, from accounting to data entry, involve repetitive tasks that easily can be handled by AI. Rather than displacing workers, however, AI algorithms function as assistants to employees. The software that makes this possible is called robotic process automation (RPA). RPAs can perform basic tasks such as checking data, completing financial transactions, and communicating between

Artificial Intelligence and You

programs. In accounting, for example, RPA can use a template to generate an invoice or other document without the worker having to enter data or adjust any settings.

Advocates of RPA point out that it allows workers to concentrate on priorities other than drudge work. Skeptics point out that, although the technology does not directly replace workers, it performs work that otherwise would have been done by humans. The loss of work hours could reduce the need for human employees. In time, as RPA becomes more sophisticated, it could cause a large-scale shift in office job descriptions as well as a possible loss of jobs.

AI is especially prevalent in certain areas of the service sector. In customer service work, for example, an inquiry may go first to a chatbot—many of which use AI—rather than a human agent. In some companies, an AI will draft a response to a customer inquiry that is

At an Amazon fulfillment center, automated robots transport goods in storage units around the facility, sparing human workers the strenuous work of lifting and carrying heavy items.

AI in the Workplace

then reviewed and edited by a human. AI can also be used to monitor a representative's job performance and suggest improvements. AI can analyze clients' activities, too. It might suggest which clients are likely to appreciate a personal pitch for a certain promotion.

Supply chain management is another area that can be significantly improved by AI. Supply chain management concerns the movement of goods and services, from the factories to store shelves. AI has improved the efficiency of factories and warehouses. RPA has the potential to streamline the complicated financial transactions involved as goods change hands. AI can also monitor quality using machine vision, predict supply and demand, anticipate equipment malfunctions, and track items being transported. Utilizing AI can help companies cut costs and improve customer satisfaction.

AI and Education

AI has the potential to make learning a lot more enjoyable and effective for both teachers and students. Teachers have notoriously heavy workloads, and AI could relieve them of some time-consuming administrative tasks. In particular, AI could help out with grading homework. Computers can already score multiple-choice tests, and AI software exists that can read and grade essays as well. The software learns to set standards by reading essays that have already been rated by human readers. Some states already use "robo-graders" to score standardized essay tests. The essay component of the Graduate Record Exam (GRE) is graded by both an AI and a human. Software utilizing AI is also effective in detecting plagiarism.

AI can provide a greater degree of personalized learning for students. Kids learn at different rates, and personalized learning would be particularly helpful for students who are struggling in a subject. Some tutoring and study programs can already interact with a student and track his or her progress during a session.

Online learning could also benefit from AI tools. Education can be made widely accessible through massive open online

Artificial Intelligence and You

In China, a robot called AI-MATHS participated in national college entrance math exams in 2017. Here, teachers review the machine's responses.

courses (MOOCs) offered by universities and other educational institutions. But studies have shown that most people who enroll in these classes fail to finish them. One computer science professor at Georgia Institute of Technology (Georgia Tech), for example, decided to experiment with boosting the engagement of the students taking his MOOC by constructing an AI teaching assistant to help answer questions.

Medical Applications

Today, medicine is increasingly seen as a data-driven field. Although some people warn about the drawbacks of losing the human element in health care, the proliferation of data offers opportunities for AI to improve processing and analysis of data. Health care is a field in which AI and medical staff can complement each other—there's no chance that AI is going to start replacing human jobs tasked with overseeing patients' well-being and lives.

Computerized medical records have already improved coordination in health care settings. AI can help organize medical records to facilitate communication among health care workers. Software has been developed that can analyze a patient's medical records to predict health problems, too, although the technology is still in early stages. AI is also well-qualified to analyze medical images and identify abnormalities. As in other fields, AI has the potential to take over some administrative tasks such as paperwork (for instance, billing and insurance-related tasks and electronic health records), allowing doctors and nurses to focus more on direct patient care.

Robots already assist doctors during highly precise robotic surgeries, such as those that use the da Vinci Surgical System. (The da Vinci Surgical System uses robotic technology that includes a magnified 3D HD vision system and tiny wristed instruments that can bend and rotate with more dexterity than a human hand.) The surgeon watches on a magnified view of the site and directs the robotic arms that complete the surgery. Because the machine can work in tight spaces, the incision is very small and heals more quickly than if it had been done by a human. In the future, AI robots may help patients and health care workers with a variety of tasks. They can help nurses lift patients, for example, and assist patients in regaining movement during rehabilitation after a stroke.

AI health care devices and apps can help monitor patients' health conditions. People can track their heart rate and blood glucose levels

Artificial Intelligence and You

A surgeon, who is not within view in this photograph, performs a minimally invasive procedure on a patient's tongue with robotic assistance by the pioneering da Vinci robot.

from home, for example. Digital assistants can remind patients to take medications.

The potential of AI goes beyond direct patient care. AI can be put to use analyzing large-scale data about factors that affect public health, for example. In drug development, AI can analyze molecular structures of potentially useful compounds as well as simulate how a newly developed drug might affect the human body.

AI in the Workplace

Hired by AI

Hiring personnel at big companies is done by the human resources (HR) department. HR managers and staff may be tasked with sorting through hundreds of applications for every job opening and selecting the best candidates. AI has proven capable of reading résumés and analyzing videos of interviews to screen for qualified candidates. It can also predict factors such as employee turnover, and some companies are even considering using AI to determine pay. Proponents of the technology point out that using algorithms to assess qualifications eliminates the problem of unconscious human bias. A 2017 Pew survey concerning automation, however, showed that most respondents were uneasy about the prospect of workers being evaluated and hired by algorithms.

The Financial World

One of the most valuable applications of AI in the realm of finance is in fraud detection. AI can use algorithms to flag transactions that don't fit in with a customer's predicted pattern of purchases. Lenders also use AI to analyze whether or not to approve an application for a loan.

AI can also help provide financial services to investors, especially smaller investors without complex assets who may not otherwise consult a human financial adviser. These "robo-advisers" are generally low-cost, automated, and managed online. They use algorithms to make investments tailored to the clients' goals and tolerance for risk.

AI can provide an advantage to Wall Street traders as well. Algorithmic trading uses AI to analyze data, identify patterns, and

Artificial Intelligence and You

decide which stocks to buy or sell. The advantage lies with the speed of the systems. Even a slight delay in making a decision can lead to a significant financial loss. Many large financial institutions are investing in AI development, and they keep the details of their AI a secret, although machine learning and deep learning are two widely used applications.

The banking industry uses AI for numerous functions. AI facilitates deposits made through mobile devices. Bank employees use robotic process automation and chatbots to improve efficiency and customer service. Automated teller machines (ATMs) were an early application of expert systems.

AI Is Watching You

Advances in AI could lead to increased levels of surveillance in public places, businesses, and even at the workplace. In the past, security cameras could theoretically watch people's every move, but in practice, there was no practical way to analyze most of the footage. Facial recognition software, however, can identify people in real time in security videos, and that's just the start of its capabilities. AI can identify people's facial expressions and postures. A camera in a semitrailer can spot a driver who is tired. A camera in an office can tell whether an employee is distracted.

In the future, employers could potentially monitor every aspect of an employee's work activity. Wearable sensors could track a worker's location and movements while a microphone picks up conversations. AI analysis of this data can make predictions about behavior. A company can use AI to determine the best length for a productive meeting, for example, or identify signs that an employee is going to leave. Online monitoring can show what documents a worker is viewing and whether he or she is communicating effectively with others. In workplaces such as factories, where safety is a concern, surveillance could confirm that workers are taking appropriate safety measures.

AI in the Workplace

A passenger undergoes verification through a facial recognition system called VeriScan as she prepares to board her plane at Dulles International Airport in Virginia.

The proliferation of AI-enhanced surveillance and monitoring could raise the issue of privacy concerns. There are few legal restrictions on surveillance in the workplace in the United States, but advances in technology could lead to a call for more privacy protections for employees. Companies will also need to consider the benefits and drawbacks of surveillance measures. AI monitoring could improve productivity and security. But it might also damage morale by making workers feel anxious and alienated.

CHAPTER 5

The Future of AI

AI is here to stay. The technology in your virtual digital assistants, targeted product recommendations, video games, fraud protection, and personal health monitoring devices has proven to be successful. AI will gradually assume more functions in the workplace as software such as robotic process automation becomes more advanced. Capabilities such as machine vision and natural language recognition will continue to make devices more user friendly.

But what about the dramatic science-fiction elements of AI, such as self-driving cars ruling the roads, or the worrisome scenarios, such as AI taking away many jobs? It's impossible to say what will come to pass. As *The Cambridge Handbook of Artificial Intelligence* points out, "If past predictions are any indication, the only thing we know today about tomorrow's science and technology is that it will be radically different from whatever we predict."

Today, even as AI grows more capable and flexible, general artificial intelligence remains in the unforeseeable future. There is no AI that approaches human-level intelligence, even as narrow AI accumulates victories against humans. Observers tend to discount landmark AI achievements after the fact. They claim that the feat, whether winning at chess or Go, isn't proof of "real" intelligence. After Watson's *Jeopardy!* victory, for example, renowned cognitive scientist Douglas Hofstadter maintained that Watson had more in common with a Google search than real intelligence.

The Future of AI

A self-driving bus called Erica—the first autonomous bus in the Spanish region of Catalonia—takes a test drive as it is introduced to the public.

Obstacles and Opportunities for AI

Experts agree on some of the ways AI is likely to evolve in the near future. Automation using AI will continue to improve efficiency. Interactive AI, such as chatbots, will facilitate communication. Other aspects and potential uses of AI are more difficult to predict.

One possible dilemma in the adoption of some AI applications is the issue of bias. You might expect that computer algorithms

Artificial Intelligence and You

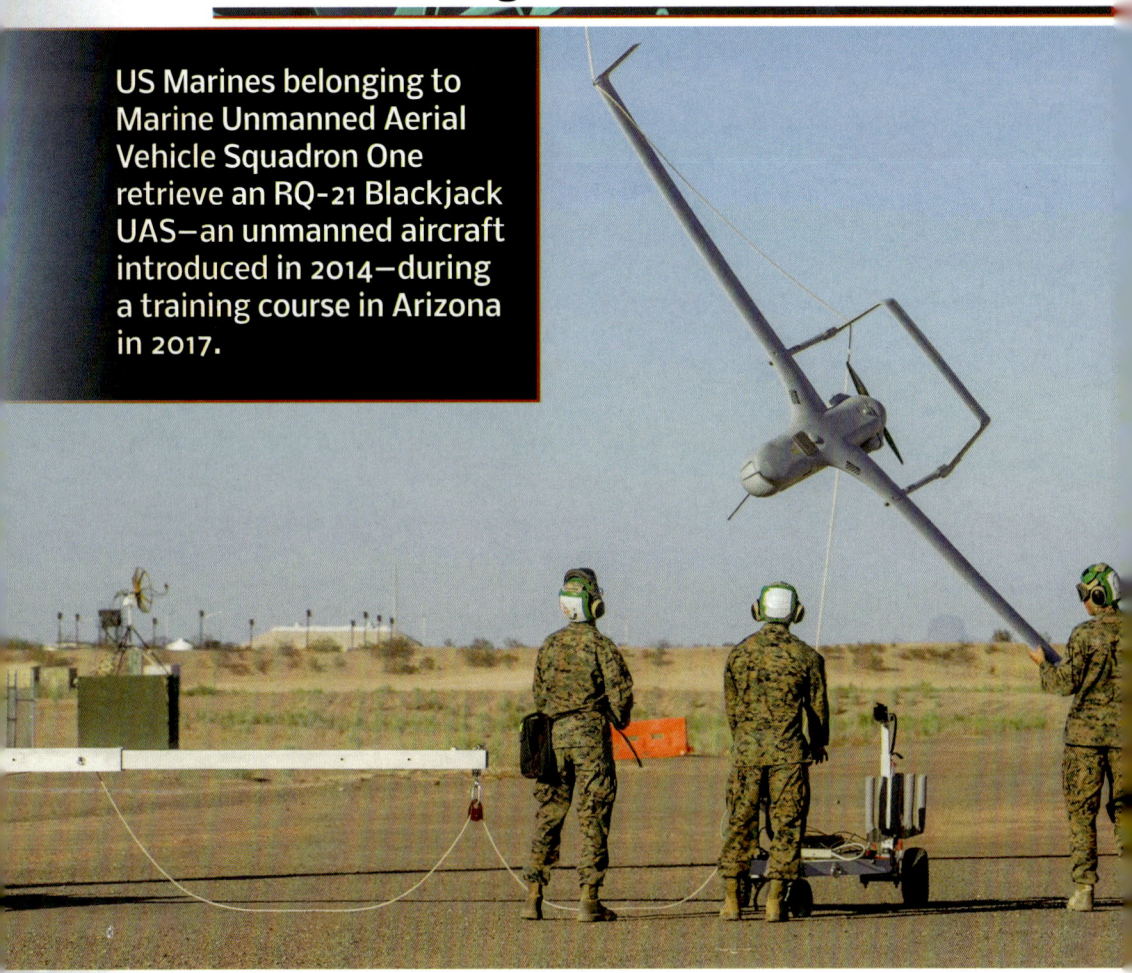

US Marines belonging to Marine Unmanned Aerial Vehicle Squadron One retrieve an RQ-21 Blackjack UAS—an unmanned aircraft introduced in 2014—during a training course in Arizona in 2017.

would be free of the psychological and emotional traits that cause bias in human beings. But AI that utilizes machine learning is fed data that teach it to make decisions. If teaching data is biased—reflecting racist or sexist attitudes, for example—the AI will reflect these biases in its output. A 2016 investigation found evidence of bias against black prisoners in an algorithm predicting which criminals were more likely to commit future crimes. Research has shown that image recognition software that has been trained by being provided with teaching images of women and men is more likely to associate women with activities such as cooking and shopping because of the inherent cultural bias in the images themselves. If AI's predictive

The Future of AI

AI in Space

The National Aeronautics and Space Administration (NASA) has long used robot technology such as probes, landers, and rovers to explore the solar system. AI could enhance the abilities of space exploration technology in a multitude of ways. AI algorithms are already being used to analyze astronomical data, such as classifying exoplanets. The company SpaceX has developed innovative reusable rockets that can land on a launchpad with the help of machine learning and other AI capabilities. In the future, AI that is incorporated into navigation systems could help spacecraft avoid debris in space. An AI system called cognitive radio could improve space communications systems. In the distant future, AI robots could explore the planets and moons of the solar system, mine asteroids for minerals, and even build structures in space.

SpaceX's Falcon Heavy rocket prepares to land on a launchpad at Cape Canaveral, Florida, in 2018. Cutting-edge technology allows the rocket to be partially reusable.

algorithms become widely adopted, tech companies must be able to guarantee that they are free of bias.

Military involvement in AI could also transform the field. Top officials in the US military support development of AI programs to counter similar efforts in China and other countries. Some tech companies, however, are uneasy about applying AI to warfare. In 2018, Google withdrew from a project that used AI to analyze footage taken by military drones. A military AI program could strengthen national security by countering potential AI threats, such as hacker attacks, fake propaganda, and fraud, including election fraud. Breakthroughs in military applications could some day be turned to nonmilitary purposes, too, benefiting society in general. But a global AI arms race could also lead to the militarization of AI and a new generation of smart weapons that could threaten world stability.

AI, the Economy, and Society

Some experts have predicted that AI is likely to transform many job categories. But will human employees continue to work alongside AI in a complementary capacity, or will AI be a truly disruptive innovation? In the past, breakthroughs such as the invention of the automobile nearly eliminated some traditional occupations—such as those dealing with horses—while creating many more categories of employment related to automobiles.

Today, AI capabilities could encroach on occupations such as paralegals, insurance underwriters, construction workers, financial analysts, drivers, accountants, and radiologists, just to name a few. If a large percentage of workers have to switch jobs because of AI, it will have profound economic and social effects. Some policy makers have raised the possibility of a universal basic income paid to all people by the government regardless of whether they work. Part

The Future of AI

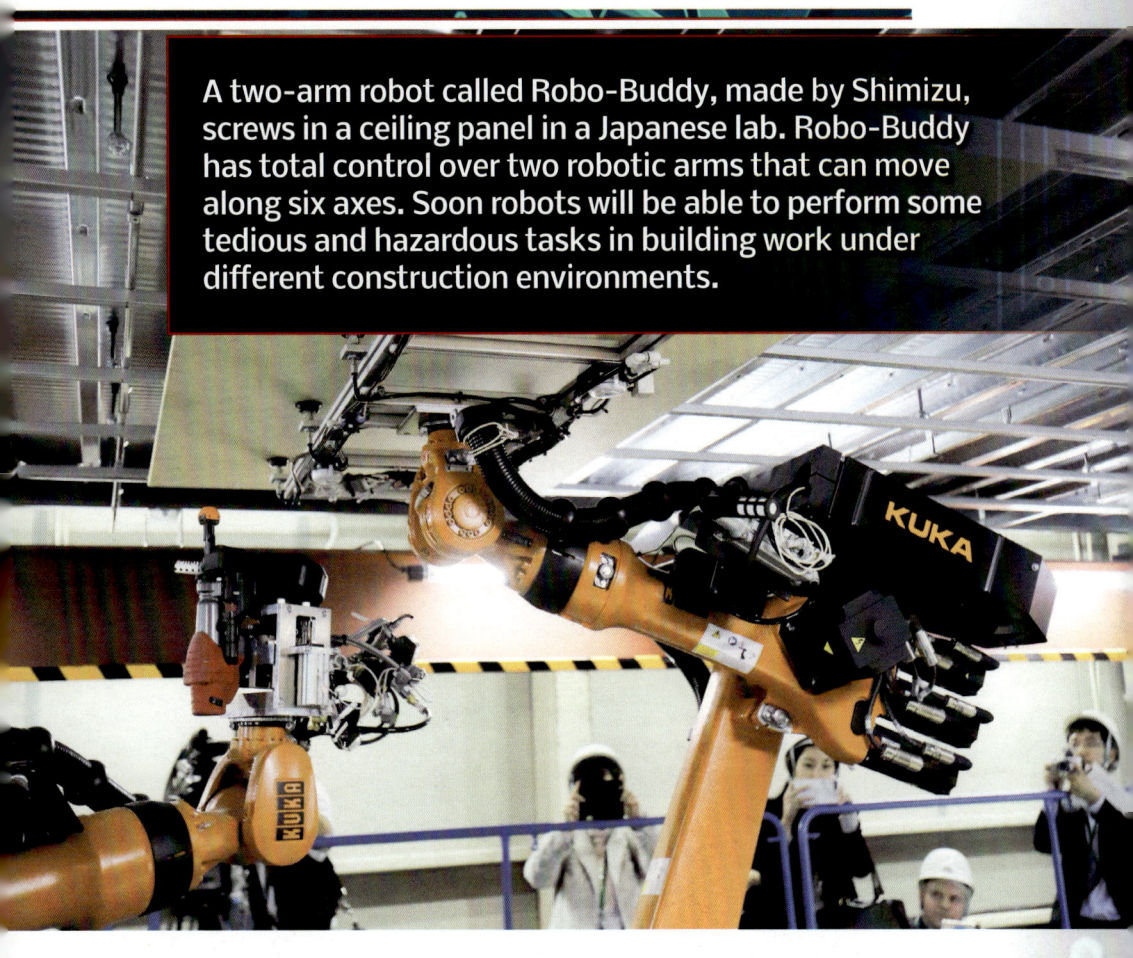

A two-arm robot called Robo-Buddy, made by Shimizu, screws in a ceiling panel in a Japanese lab. Robo-Buddy has total control over two robotic arms that can move along six axes. Soon robots will be able to perform some tedious and hazardous tasks in building work under different construction environments.

of the rationale behind the concept is the possibility of widespread elimination of jobs because of automation.

In the 2017 Pew survey about automation, a majority of respondents believed that policies should limit automation and address its effects on society. There have been calls for regulation regarding many other areas related to AI. A few of these issues include transparency concerning potentially biased algorithms; protection of private data; determining who is legally responsible for the consequences of an AI's actions; establishing standards for AI development and testing; and requiring chatbots to state that they're not human. The tech industry remains wary of regulations that could stifle innovation, but the field is growing and changing so rapidly that it is outpacing any policies that could hold AI accountable.

The Singularity and Beyond

In the 1980s, futurist Vernor Vinge coined the term "technological singularity," a concept that describes the creation of an AI superintelligence that fundamentally transforms human civilization. Many futurists and AI experts have addressed whether the singularity could truly occur and how it would unfold.

The singularity is highly speculative. Today, researchers have made little progress on achieving artificial general intelligence, much less creating AI that could be a precursor to an intelligence far beyond human scope. Some AI experts warn that discussion of runaway AI intelligence creates a distraction from more conceivable likely threats posed by AI. Nonetheless, the singularity remains a fascinating topic of debate.

The most famous conjecture regarding the singularity is futurist Ray Kurzweil's prediction that it will arrive in 2045. Kurzweil sees the postsingularity age as a time of explosive progress, in which humans could potentially eliminate the process of aging and merge with computers and robots. A drastically opposing view is the AI apocalypse scenario, in which a superintelligence subjugates or even destroys humanity. The opinionated tech entrepreneur Elon Musk has speculated publicly about "a fleet of artificial intelligence-enhanced robots capable of destroying mankind" as quoted in *Vanity Fair* in 2017. He has also raised the concern that a global AI arms race could lead to World War III.

On the other hand, computer scientist Andrew Ng has famously compared the singularity to the danger of overpopulation on Mars. It might happen someday, but humans won't have to worry about the possibility for a long time.

Glossary

algorithm A step-by-step set of rules for solving a problem, especially in mathematics or computing.

automation The use of machines, especially equipment with advanced technology, to do work in manufacturing or other production processes.

autonomous Capable of moving without direct human control.

bias A preference or prejudice that is often unconscious or preconceived.

closed-circuit television (CCTV) A TV system in which cameras send video signals to a certain number of monitors for the purpose of security surveillance.

cognition The mental activities that include thinking, knowing or understanding, remembering, and learning.

database An organized set of data in a computer system that can be easily searched and updated.

demographics Statistical data, such as that categorized by age, income, gender, race, location, and so forth, that refer to the population and specific groups within it.

drone An unmanned aircraft that is controlled remotely by humans or navigates itself autonomously.

ethical Pertaining to behavior that is considered correct or moral.

exoplanet A planet beyond the solar system.

fraud The crime of using trickery or deception for money or some other personal gain.

Artificial Intelligence and You

hype The use of a great deal of promotion or publicity for a product to get people interested in that product.

implication A possible consequence or effect of a decision or an action.

innovation Something new, such as a technological development or product.

interactive In electronic communications, allowing a two-way flow of information between the device and the user.

lidar A detection system, similar to radar, that uses pulsed laser light rather than microwaves to determine properties of objects.

linguistics The scientific study of language.

neural Relating to a nerve cell or the nervous system of the body.

precursor Predecessor or forerunner.

productivity The value of output compared with the value of input, especially in industry.

program Coded operations performed by a computer, or to write these operations.

proliferation The quick increase in the amount or number of something.

robot A machine capable of performing specific preprogrammed functions or tasks.

scenario A projected or imagined sequence of events.

sensor A device that detects physical properties such as heat or the vital signs of the human body.

Glossary

software The programs used to operate computers and related devices.

speculative Based on conjecture rather than fact; hypothetical.

statistics The field related to the collection, organization, analysis, and interpretation of large amounts of numerical data.

surveillance Close observation or monitoring, such as of a particular site or group of people.

For More Information

Artificial Intelligence Society (AIS)

Website: https://aisutd.org
contact@aisutd.org
Facebook: @AIS UTD
Twitter: @ais_utd
AIS is an organization based at the University of Texas at Dallas that tries to make the artificial intelligence field easy to understand by reaching out to people to explain AI's impact on and benefits to the world. AIS holds workshops and visits high schools in Dallas and Houston in its K-12 outreach program.

Association for the Advancement of Artificial Intelligence (AAAI)

2275 East Bayshore Road, Suite 160
Palo Alto, CA 94303
(650) 328-3123
Website: https://www.aaai.org
Facebook: AAAI - Association for the Advancement of Artificial Intelligence
Twitter: @RealAAAI
The Association for the Advancement of Artificial Intelligence is a nonprofit organization that supports scientific research into AI and educates the public about the science of AI and its development.

For More Information

Canada Science and Technology Museum

2421 Lancaster Road
Ottawa, ON K1G 5A3
Canada
(866) 442-4416
Website: https://ingeniumcanada.org/cstm
Facebook and Twitter: @SciTechMuseum
The Canada Science and Technology Museum offers interactive exhibitions related to Canadian science, technology, and innovation.

Canadian Institute for Advanced Research (CIFAR)

MaRS Centre, West Tower
661 University Avenue, Suite 505
Toronto, ON M5G 1M1
Canada
(416) 971-4251
Website: https://www.cifar.ca
The Canadian Institute for Advanced Research is a research institute that supports programs in AI and other areas of cutting-edge technology.

Computer History Museum

1401 North Shoreline Boulevard
Mountain View, CA 94043
(650) 810-1010
Website: http://www.computerhistory.org

Artificial Intelligence and You

Facebook and Instagram: @computerhistory
Twitter: @ComputerHistory
The Computer History Museum explores the history of computing and its continued impact on society.

Defense Advanced Research Projects Agency (DARPA)

675 North Randolph Street
Arlington, VA 22203-2114
(703) 526-6630
Website: https://www.darpa.mil
Facebook and Twitter: @DARPA
The Defense Advanced Research Projects Agency is the military agency that supports the development of cutting-edge technological innovations vital to national security.

Miraikan–The National Museum of Emerging Science and Innovation

2-3-6 Aomi, Koto-ku
Tokyo 135-0064
Japan
+81-3-3570-9151
Website: http://www.miraikan.jst.go.jp/en/
Facebook: @miraikan.en
Instagram and Twitter: @miraikan
Miraikan offers permanent and rotating exhibits related to science and technology, holds events such as public lectures, and serves as a research institution. The museum includes AI-related exhibits such as "Robots in Your Life" and "Android: What Is Human?"

For More Information

MIT Computer Science & Artificial Intelligence Laboratory

32 Vassar Street
Cambridge, MA 02139
(617) 253-5851
Website: https://www.csail.mit.edu
Facebook: @MITCSAIL
Instagram: @mit_csail
Twitter: @MIT_CSAIL
The Computer Science & Artificial Intelligence Laboratory at MIT educates students and performs cutting-edge research in many areas of computer science, robotics, and AI.

Science Museum

Exhibition Road
South Kensington
London SW7 2DD
United Kingdom
0333 241 4000
Facebook: @sciencemuseumlondon
Instagram and Twitter: @sciencemuseum
Website: https://sciencemuseum.org.uk
The Science Museum holds exhibitions about significant scientific and technological inventions and their interesting stories. These include robotics and artificial intelligence and their impact around the world.

For Further Reading

Allen, John. *What Is the Future of Artificial Intelligence?* San Diego, CA: ReferencePoint Press, Inc., 2017.

Bond, Dave. *Artificial Intelligence.* Broomall, PA: Mason Crest, 2017.

Brockman, John, ed. *What to Think About Machines That Think.* New York, NY: Harper Perennial, 2015.

Cooper, James. *Inside Robotics.* New York, NY: Rosen Publishing, 2019.

Gibbs, Nancy, ed. *Artificial Intelligence: The Future of Humankind.* TIME Special Edition. New York, NY: Time Books, 2017.

Hogan, Christa C. *How Artificial Intelligence Will Impact Society.* San Diego, CA: ReferencePoint Press, Inc., 2019.

Hulick, Kathryn. *Artificial Intelligence.* Minneapolis, MN: ABDO Publishing, 2016.

McPherson, Stephanie Sammartino. *Artificial Intelligence: Building Smarter Machines.* Minneapolis, MN: Twenty-First Century Books, 2018.

Porterfield, Jason. *Robots, Cyborgs, and Androids.* New York, NY: Rosen Publishing, 2019.

Reese, Byron. *The Fourth Age: Smart Robots, Conscious Computers, and the Future of Humanity.* New York, NY: Atria Books, 2018.

Walsh, Toby. *Machines That Think: The Future of Artificial Intelligence.* Amherst, NY: Prometheus Books, 2018.

Bibliography

Brundage, Miles, and Joanna Bryson. "Why Watson Is Real Artificial Intelligence." Slate, February 14, 2014. http://www.slate.com/blogs/future_tense/2014/02/14/watson_is_real_artificial_intelligence_despite_claims_to_the_contrary.html.

Davies, Alex. "The *WIRED* Guide to Self-Driving Cars." *WIRED*, February 1, 2018. https://www.wired.com/story/guide-self-driving-cars.

Dellot, Benedict, and Fabian Wallace-Stephens. "What Is the Difference Between AI & Robotics?" Medium, September 17, 2017. https://medium.com/@thersa/what-is-the-difference-between-ai-robotics-d93715b4ba7f.

Dowd, Maureen. "Elon Musk's Billion-Dollar Crusade to Stop the A.I. Apocalypse." *Vanity Fair*, March 26, 2017. https://www.vanityfair.com/news/2017/03/elon-musk-billion-dollar-crusade-to-stop-ai-space-x.

The Economist. "Special Report on Artificial Intelligence." March 31, 2018.

Frankish, Keith, and William M. Ramsey, eds. *The Cambridge Handbook of Artificial Intelligence*. Cambridge, UK: University Printing House, 2015.

Grossman, Lev. "2045: The Year Man Becomes Immortal." *TIME*, February 10, 2011. http://content.time.com/time/magazine/article/0,9171,2048299-1,00.html.

Horaczek, Stan. "Here's Where Your New Car Lands on the Self-driving Scale." *Popular Science*, January 17, 2018. https://www.popsci.com/self-driving-car-scale.

Howell, Elizabeth. "NASA's Space AI Hunts Exoplanets, Not Humans—Yet." Space.com, May 27, 2018. https://www.space.com/40711-artificial-intelligence-space-and-humanity.html.

Husain, Amir. *The Sentient Machine: The Coming Age of Artificial Intelligence.* New York, NY: Scribner, 2017.

Kaplan, Jerry. *Artificial Intelligence: What Everyone Should Know.* New York, NY: Oxford University Press, 2016.

Kaplan, Jerry. *Humans Need Not Apply: A Guide to Wealth and Work in the Age of Artificial Intelligence.* New Haven, CT: Yale University Press, 2015.

Leopold, Todd. "A Professor Built an AI Teaching Assistant for His Courses—and It Could Shape the Future of Education." Business Insider, March 22, 2017. https://www.businessinsider.com/a-professor-built-an-ai-teaching-assistant-for-his-courses-and-it-could-shape-the-future-of-education-2017-3.

Lohr, Steve. "'The Beginning of a Wave': A.I. Tiptoes into the Workplace." *New York Times,* August 5, 2018.

Lou, Harbing. "Artificial Intelligence AI in Video Games: Toward a More Intelligent Game." Harvard University Graduate School of Arts and Sciences, August 28, 2017. http://sitn.hms.harvard.edu/flash/2017/ai-video-games-toward-intelligent-game.

McCarthy, John. "John McCarthy's Home Page." Retrieved August 29, 2018. http://www-formal.stanford.edu/jmc/index.html.

Metz, Cade. "As Pentagon Turns to A.I., Will Big Tech Lend Hand?" *New York Times,* August 27, 2018. Page B1.

Mueller, John Paul, and Luca Massaron. *Artificial Intelligence for Dummies.* Hoboken, NJ: John Wiley and Sons, Inc., 2018.

Bibliography

Narula, Gautam. "Everyday Examples of Artificial Intelligence and Machine Learning." TechEmergence, July 22, 2018. https://www.techemergence.com/everyday-examples-of-ai.

Naughton, John. "Even Algorithms Are Biased Against Black Men." *Guardian*, June 26, 2016. https://www.theguardian.com/commentisfree/2016/jun/26/algorithms-racial-bias-offenders-florida.

O'Brien, Matt. "How Much All-seeing AI Surveillance Is Too Much?" Phys.org, July 3, 2018. https://phys.org/news/2018-07-all-seeing-ai-surveillance.html.

Olmstead, Kenneth. "Nearly Half of Americans Use Digital Voice Assistants, Mostly on Their Smartphones." Pew Research Center, December 12, 2017. http://www.pewresearch.org/fact-tank/2017/12/12/nearly-half-of-americans-use-digital-voice-assistants-mostly-on-their-smartphones.

Parker, Clifton B. "Artificial Intelligence Will Both Disrupt and Benefit the Workplace, Stanford Scholar Says." *Stanford News*, May 17, 2018. https://news.stanford.edu/2018/05/17/artificial-intelligence-workplace.

Simonite, Tom. "The *WIRED* Guide to Artificial Intelligence." *WIRED*, February 1, 2018. https://www.wired.com/story/guide-artificial-intelligence.

Smith, Aaron, and Monica Anderson. "Automation in Everyday Life." Pew Research Center, October 4, 2017. http://www.pewinternet.org/2017/10/04/automation-in-everyday-life.

Smith, Tovia. "More States Opting To 'Robo-Grade' Student Essays by Computer." NPR, June 30, 2018. https://www.npr.org/2018/06/30/624373367/more-states-opting-to-robo-grade-student-essays-by-computer.

Sparks, Sarah D. "How 'Intelligent' Tutors Could Transform Teaching." Education Week, September 26, 2017. https://www.edweek.org/ew/articles/2017/09/27/how-intelligent-tutors-could-transform-teaching.html.

Statt, Nick. "AI Is Google's Secret Weapon for Remaking Its Oldest and Most Popular Apps." Verge, May 10, 2018. https://www.theverge.com/2018/5/10/17340004/google-ai-maps-news-secret-weapon-remaking-old-apps-products-io-2018.

Tegmark, Max. *Life 3.0: Being Human in the Age of Artificial Intelligence*. New York, NY: Alfred A. Knopf, 2017.

Vincent, James. "AI and Robots Will Destroy Fewer Jobs than Previously Feared, Says New OECD Report." Verge, April 3, 2018. https://www.theverge.com/2018/4/3/17192002/ai-job-loss-predictions-forecasts-automation-oecd-report.

Vincent, James. "What Counts as Artificially Intelligent? AI and Deep Learning, Explained." The Verge, February 29, 2016. https://www.theverge.com/2016/2/29/11133682/deep-learning-ai-explained-machine-learning.

Walravens, Samantha. "How This Teen Is Using Artificial Intelligence to Stop Gun Violence." *Forbes*, May 3, 2018. https://www.forbes.com/sites/geekgirlrising/2018/05/03/how-this-teen-is-using-artificial-intelligence-to-stop-gun-violence/#6428d4a3526e.

Warwick, Kevin. *Artificial Intelligence: The Basics*. New York, NY: Routledge, 2012.

Index

A
Advanced Research Projects Agency Network (ARPANET), 20
Alexa, 24
algorithms, bias in, 5, 43–44
AlphaGo, 4, 9
Aphrodite, 16
artificial general intelligence (AGI), 9
artificial intelligence
  advances to come, 42–48
  history of, 4, 16–23
  pros and cons of, 12–15
  uses in daily life, 4, 9–10, 24–25, 27–32
  what it is, 4, 7–12
  workplace uses, 5, 11, 12–14, 33–41
automatic braking, 28

B
baby monitors, 27
banking, 40

C
Carnegie Mellon University, 18
chess, 4, 9, 21, 27, 42
cognitive radio, 45
collision avoidance technology, 28
customer service, 34–35

D
Dartmouth Workshop, 17, 18, 19
da Vinci Surgical System, 37
Deep Blue, 4, 9, 12, 21
deep learning, 9, 23
Defense Advanced Research Projects Agency (DARPA), 20, 23
DENDRAL, 20
digital assistants, 24–25, 30, 32, 38, 42
drones, 12, 14, 46

E
ELIZA, 20
expert system, creation of first, 20

F
facial recognition software, 5, 7, 14, 25, 27, 40
factories, use of AI in, 12, 13
fraud detection, 39

G
Galatea (myth), 16
Galatea (novel), 16
Go, 4, 27, 42
Google Maps, 30
grading, 35

61

H

Harnad, Stevan, 10
Hofstadter, Douglas, 42
human resources, replacing with AI, 39

I

information theory, 18
Instagram, 27
internet of things (IoT), 30

J

Jeopardy!, 4, 7, 21, 42

K

Kasparov, Gary, 3, 21
Kurzweil, Ray, 48

L

linguistic ability, 7, 18, 20
LinkedIn, 27
LISP, 17
Logical Theorist, 18

M

machine learning, what it is, 21–23, 24, 44
mapping, 30
Massachusetts Institute of Technology (MIT), 18, 20, 21
McCarthy, John, 4, 17, 18

medical field, use of AI in, 12, 37–38
Minsky, Marvin, 18, 21

N

National Aeronautics and Space Administration (NASA), 45
natural language processing, 10
neural networks, 9, 18, 19, 21, 23
Newell, Allen, 18

O

output layer, 23

P

Papert, Seymour, 21
perceptron, 19, 21
plagiarism detection, 35
Powers, Richard 16
processing nodes, 23
Pygmalion, 16

R

reinforcement learning, 23
robotic arms, 7
robotic process automation (RPA), 33–34, 42
robotics, 10–12
Rochester, Nathaniel, 18
Rosenblatt, Frank, 19

Index

S
self-driving cars, 5, 12, 13, 14, 23, 28–29, 42
self-reflection, 8
Selfridge, Oliver, 18
Shakey, 20, 21
Shannon, Claude, 18
SHRDLU, 21
Simon, Herbert, 18, 19
singularity, 15, 48
Siri, 24
smart grid, 31
smart homes, 30, 32
social robots, 28
Stanford Artificial Intelligence Laboratory, 18
stock trading, 39–40
supervised learning, 22, 23
supply chain management, 35
surveillance, 14, 40–41

symbolic reasoning, 9

T
targeted ads, 27
Total Turing Test, 10
Turing, Alan, 10
Turing test, 10

U
Uber, 14
unsupervised learning, 22, 23

V
Vinge, Vernor, 48

W
Watson, 4, 7, 8, 9, 12, 21, 42
weak versus strong AI, 9
Weizenbaum, Joseph, 19–20
Winograd, Terry, 21

Artificial Intelligence and You

About the Author

Corona Brezina has written numerous books for young adults. Several of her previous works have also focused on topics related to science and technology, including *Time Travel* (Sci-Fi or STEM?); *Careers in Nanotechnology* (Cutting-Edge Careers); *Top STEM Careers in Math* (Cutting-Edge STEM Careers); and *Discovering Relativity* (The Scientist's Guide to Physics). She lives in Chicago, Illinois.

Photo Credits

Cover (artificial brain and lower background) Oliver Burston/Ikon Images/Getty Images; pp. 4–5 Ben Hider/Getty Images; pp. 6, 8, 11, 34 Bloomberg/Getty Images; p. 13 Justin Sullivan/Getty Images; pp. 16–17, 29, 31 © AP Images; p. 19 Frederic Lewis/Archive Photos/Getty Images; p. 22 Jim Wilson/The New York Times/Redux; p. 25 Juan Ci/Shutterstock.com; p. 26 Roy Rochlin/FilmMagic/Getty Images; p. 36 China News Service/Visual China Group/Getty Images; p. 38 WPA Pool/Getty Images; p. 41 Jim Watson/AFP/Getty Images; p. 43 Josep Lago/AFP/Getty Images; p. 44 U.S. Marine Corps photo by Lance Cpl. Rhita Daniel; p. 45 (inset) NASA/Kim Shiflett; p. 47 Aflo Co. Ltd./Alamy Stock Photo; cover and interior pages background image (circuit board) jijomathai/Shutterstock.com; additional interior pages circuit board image gandroni/Shutterstock.com.

Design/Layout: Brian Garvey; Senior Editor: Kathy Kuhtz Campbell; Photo Researcher: Nicole DiMella